Los Angeles

Los Angeles

A Downtown America Book

Cheryl Zach

Dillon Press, Inc. Minneapolis, MN 55415

For my husband Chuck,
with love and gratitude

Photographic Acknowledgments

The photographs are reproduced through the courtesy of the California Historical Society/Ticor Title Insurance, Los Angeles (pages 21, 23, 24); Greater Los Angeles Visitor's and Convention Bureau; McDonnell Douglas; Planning Department, City of Los Angeles (cover, 10, 18, 43, 54); Rockwell International; Universal Studios; Charles Van Pelt (pages 2, 15, 46, 49); and Cheryl Zach. Special thanks to Kenneth C. Topping, General Manager and Director of Planning, City of Los Angeles.

Library of Congress Cataloging-in-Publication Data

Zach, Cheryl.
    Los Angeles / by Cheryl Zach.
        p.   cm. — (A Downtown America book)
    Includes index.
    Summary: Describes the past and present, neighborhoods, historic sites, attractions, and festivals of Los Angeles.
    ISBN 0-87518-415-4 : $12.95
    1. Los Angeles (Calif.)—Juvenile literature. [1. Los Angeles (Calif.)] I. Title. II. Series.
F869.L84Z33 1989
979.4'94—dc 20   89-12024
                                                              CIP
                                                              AC

Dillon Press, Inc., 242 Portland Avenue South
Minneapolis, Minnesota 55415

Printed in the United States of America
1 2 3 4 5 6 7 8 9 10 98 97 96 95 94 93 92 91 90 89

About the Author

Cheryl Zach is a free-lance writer and former teacher who lives in the Los Angeles area. The author of sixteen books for young people, she crisscrossed the City of Angels and talked to many people to prepare for writing this book. Ms. Zach is a member of the Society of Children's Book Writers, the California Writers' Club, and P.E.N.

Contents

Fast Facts about Los Angeles

Los Angeles: The City of Angels, the Southland

Location: Southern California coast, 130 miles (209 kilometers) north of the United States/Mexico border, bounded by the Angeles National Forest to the northwest, Ventura County to the west, and Orange County to the east

Area: City, 467 square miles (1,214 square kilometers); consolidated metropolitan area, 34,181 square miles (88,528 square kilometers)

Population (1988 estimate): City, 3,361,597; consolidated metropolitan area, 12,372,586

Major Population Groups: Whites, Hispanics (Latinos), Blacks, and Asians

Altitude: Highest—5,080 feet (1,550 meters); lowest—sea level

Climate: Average mean temperature is 83°F (28°C) in summer, 65°F (18°C) in winter; average annual precipitation, including rain and snow, is 15 inches (38 centimeters); rainy season lasts from November to March or April, with a 14-inch average rainfall during this time; city is known for its mild, sunny climate

Founding Date: 1781; incorporated as a city in 1850

City Flag: City seal in center of three vertical jagged stripes—green for vegetation, yellow for grapes, and orange for citrus crops

City Seal: Shield inside a circle; shield is four parts, each symbolizing Los Angeles under different rulers: crowned lion, rampant, and castle, Spain; eagle grasping serpent in beak, Mexico; Grizzly bear and star, California Republic; stars and stripes, United States

Form of Government: Mayor-council; mayor oversees law enforcement, appoints city officers, supervises departments, and prepares the budget; council passes legislation and approves the budget; both mayor and council are elected to four-year-terms; Los Angeles is one of the few metropolitan areas in the country to have an area-wide government

Important Industries: Aerospace, entertainment, electronics, oil, finance, tourism, engineering, chemicals; Los Angeles is the largest manufacturing center in the United States

Festivals and Parades

January: Tournament of Roses Parade and Rose Bowl, Pasadena

January/February: Chinese New Year and Golden Dragon parade

March: Return of the Swallows, San Juan Capistrano

April: Renaissance Pleasure Faire; Toyota Grand Prix, Long Beach

May: Cinco de Mayo

July: International Surf Festival, South Bay cities

August: Nisei Week, Little Tokyo

September: Los Angeles County Fair, Pomono

November: Hollywood Christmas parade; Doo-dah parade, Pasadena

December: Las Posadas (Mexican Christmas festival); Los Angeles Harbor Christmas Afloat

For further information about festivals and parades, see agencies listed on page 57.

United States

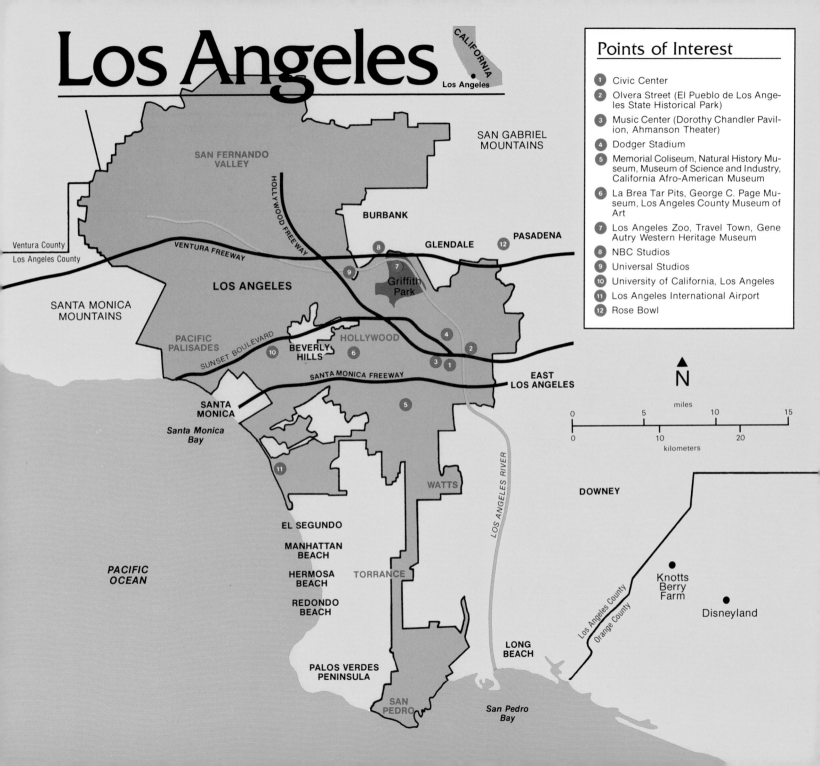

Los Angeles

CALIFORNIA
Los Angeles

Points of Interest

1. Civic Center
2. Olvera Street (El Pueblo de Los Angeles State Historical Park)
3. Music Center (Dorothy Chandler Pavilion, Ahmanson Theater)
4. Dodger Stadium
5. Memorial Coliseum, Natural History Museum, Museum of Science and Industry, California Afro-American Museum
6. La Brea Tar Pits, George C. Page Museum, Los Angeles County Museum of Art
7. Los Angeles Zoo, Travel Town, Gene Autry Western Heritage Museum
8. NBC Studios
9. Universal Studios
10. University of California, Los Angeles
11. Los Angeles International Airport
12. Rose Bowl

SAN GABRIEL MOUNTAINS

SAN FERNANDO VALLEY

HOLLYWOOD FREEWAY

BURBANK

GLENDALE

PASADENA

Ventura County
Los Angeles County

VENTURA FREEWAY

LOS ANGELES

SANTA MONICA MOUNTAINS

Griffith Park

PACIFIC PALISADES

SUNSET BOULEVARD

BEVERLY HILLS

HOLLYWOOD

SANTA MONICA FREEWAY

EAST LOS ANGELES

SANTA MONICA

Santa Monica Bay

▲ N

miles
0   5   10   15
0   10   20
kilometers

WATTS

LOS ANGELES RIVER

DOWNEY

EL SEGUNDO

MANHATTAN BEACH

HERMOSA BEACH

TORRANCE

REDONDO BEACH

PACIFIC OCEAN

Knotts Berry Farm

Disneyland

Los Angeles County
Orange County

LONG BEACH

PALOS VERDES PENINSULA

SAN PEDRO

San Pedro Bay

1

City of Many Faces

When you think Los Angeles, think big! From the air, this southern California giant appears as mile after mile of city blocks. At night, the city's bright yellow and white lights seem to stretch as far as the eye can see.

Los Angeles has almost every kind of geography. The City of Angels sprawls across a coastal basin, with the Pacific Ocean to the west and south, the Santa Monica Mountains within its city limits, the San Gabriel Mountains to the northeast, and vast deserts only a few hours away. Residents of Los Angeles, called Angelenos, can drive to the beach to swim or surf, hike in the Angeles National Forest in the summer, or ski down a snowy mountain slope in the winter.

Once a sleepy Mexican village, Los Angeles is now the second-largest U.S. city after New York. It has more

Downtown Los Angeles at night.

The Los Angeles skyline with Mount Wilson and the San Gabriel Mountains in the background.

than 3 million people within its 467 square miles (1,214 square kilometers). In 1989 Los Angeles replaced New York as the nation's largest metropolitan area. The metropolitan area is made up of the city and the suburbs that are located around it.

In some ways Los Angeles is also a city of many cities. Los Angeles County includes 80 separate cities, squeezed tightly together. On the map, the county looks like an odd-shaped patchwork quilt. In real life, Angelenos can walk from one city to another simply by crossing a street. On one side they might be standing in Santa Monica, and on the other, Pacific Palisades. Only the street signs show in which city or community they are located.

Los Angeles is also a city of many faces—an international city—and has been since its beginning. Walking through downtown, a visitor can hear many foreign languages and accents. Angelenos who form the city's largest and most prominent ethnic group are called Latinos—immigrants or descendants of immigrants from Mexico or other Latin American countries. As a result, Spanish is Los Angeles's second language.

Asian Americans, too, make up an important part of the city's population. Chinese, Filipinos, Japanese, and Koreans form major ethnic groups. During the 1980s, many new immigrants arrived from Southeast Asia, including refugees from Cambodia, Laos, and Vietnam, as well as

Mexican-American girls on Olvera Street during the Cinco de Mayo celebration.

Members of a high school band help celebrate black history month at City Hall.

thousands of refugees from Central America.

Along with the large Latino and Asian groups, many African Americans live in Los Angeles. By the end of this century, the Anglos—white Americans of European descent—will be a minority. The city's many ethnic groups make it a truly international community.

As more and more people have come to Los Angeles, it has grown outward to cover a huge urban area. One reason that the city has grown

Hollywood and Harbor freeways in Los Angeles.

out and not just up—although there are tall buildings downtown—is the famous Los Angeles network of freeways. More than 30 multi-laned highways crisscross the Los Angeles area and move millions of people every day.

Los Angeles has been called a city of cars. Cars crowd its streets and fill the freeways. In fact, Angelenos own more cars per person than the people of any other city in the world.

But the use of so many automobiles has also caused some of the city's worst problems. Exhaust fumes from cars, trucks, and buses are the main component of the ugly, unhealthful air pollution, called smog, that often hangs in brown layers over the coastal basin. The surrounding mountains act as barriers that can trap the smog over the city.

To help solve the problem, the city decided to build a modern mass transit system. Construction began on Metro Rail in September 1986. Electric powered, this high-speed rail rapid transit is similar to systems in Washington, D.C., and Atlanta. One line running west and north will link downtown with the San Fernando Valley. Another line will connect Norwalk, in eastern Los Angeles County, with El Segundo, near the ocean. Five

stations will include one at Union Station, the city's historic train terminal. Metro Rail should begin operation in 1993 and carry 55,000 passengers by the end of the century.

Traffic is brisk in the air as well as on the ground. Los Angeles International Airport (L.A.X.) is one of the world's busiest—third largest in passenger traffic, and second in cargo traffic. L.A.X. serves 67 major airlines with eight multi-level terminals.

In addition to smog and traffic congestion, other problems native to southern California are even more unpredictable. In late summer and fall, hot, dry Santa Anna winds blow out of the desert. They fan the parched countryside, causing dangerous brush fires in outlying areas.

Other natural dangers lie deep underground. The San Andreas Fault is a crack in the earth's crust. It marks the boundary between two of the "plates" that cover the earth and fit together like the pieces of a giant jigsaw puzzle. When the earth's plates suddenly shift along the places where they meet, earthquakes occur. The San Andreas Fault runs through the Los Angeles area, along with more than a dozen smaller faults.

Angelenos are accustomed to the shaking caused by small earthquakes. In 1971 a much stronger earthquake centered in San Fernando killed 64 people and damaged many buildings. Residents are urged to keep emergency supplies on hand; emergency services practice frequent earthquake drills, and building codes are strict. The city wants to be prepared for the "big one" that experts expect by the end of the twentieth century.

Even with these dangers, thousands of people move to the Los Angeles area every year, drawn by its warm, sunny climate and healthy local economy. The now huge City of Angels continues a remarkable period of rapid growth that began little more than a century ago.

2

City of Angels

How did a tiny Mexican town grow into a sprawling metropolis? How did skyscrapers come to stand on the site of a native American village? Los Angeles has a long and fascinating history.

Four hundred years ago, Gabrielino Indians lived in a village called Yang-na, near what is now downtown Los Angeles. The first European made the long sea journey to the New World's western shores in 1542. Juan Rodríguez Cabrillo, a Portuguese adventurer hired by Spain, added Yang-na to his map as he surveyed the California coastline. Spain later began to colonize the area, building missions in Baja (lower) California, and then moving north.

In 1769 Gaspar de Portolá, a captain in the Spanish army, and Juan Crespi, a priest, stopped at Yang-na

Gabrielino Indians once lived along the Los Angeles River near what is now downtown Los Angeles.

on their way to Monterey Bay. Crespi noted in his journal that Yang-na was a "delightful place." The two men named the area *Nuestra Señora la Reina de Los Ángeles de Porciúncula*, or Our Lady the Queen of the Angels of Porciúncula—the name of a chapel in Italy connected with Crespi's Franciscan order.

In 1781 the Spanish governor of California, Felipe de Neve, offered free land and supplies to people willing to settle the "delightful place." That February, 11 families from northern Mexico began the long journey by horseback or mule, arriving at last in September. They founded the *pueblo* (town) of Our Lady the Queen of Angels. Included in their group were Spanish, Indian, white, and black settlers.

By 1800 Los Angeles had more than three hundred people, who raised huge herds of long-horned cattle on vast ranches. In 1821 Mexico became an independent country. Los Angeles served part of the time as the capital of Alto (higher) California, a Mexican province.

The first white man to come overland to California was Jedediah Smith, a fur trapper who arrived in 1826. By the 1840s, more American settlers crossed the mountains and plains in long wagon trains. Although Mexican residents still outnumbered these newcomers, the "Yankees" continued to come.

Interested in this rich new land, the United States tried to buy Cali-

This drawing shows the arrival of Jedediah Smith at Mission San Gabriel.

fornia from Mexico, but Mexico refused. Because of this and other conflicts, the two nations stopped talking and started fighting in 1846. During the war, U.S. troops occupied Los Angeles on two occasions.

In 1848 Mexico surrendered and signed a treaty giving California to the United States. When Los Angeles was incorporated as a city on April 4, 1850—the same year California became a state—its population was 1,610. Over the next 20 years, the city grew slowly.

But a new pathway to the West was about to open. Thousands of workers had been busy building a transcontinental railroad, which crossed the entire country from east to west. In May 1869, the last spike was driven. Now Americans could travel much more quickly and easily to California, and in 1876—when the Southern Pacific Railroad linked Los Angeles to San Francisco—on to the City of Angels.

Nine years later, the Santa Fe Railroad built a rail line straight through the Southwest to Los Angeles. By the next year, because of rate wars between competing railroads, passengers could travel from Chicago to Los Angeles for fares as low as one dollar! Now whole trains full of people arrived daily.

In 1899 the city started construction on a harbor at San Pedro. It was finished in 1914, the same year as the Panama Canal, making Los Angeles an important port. About the same

Railroad cars haul large rocks for the breakwater of the Los Angeles harbor at San Pedro in 1899.

time, rich new oil fields were discovered, and the already busy oil industry began to boom.

Another natural resource, Los Angeles's mild climate, drew early filmmakers west. The first silent films would make Hollywood a world-famous name even before the moviemakers began to produce "talkies." And the same delightful weather attracted many tourists to the area's beaches and orange groves.

The future looked bright. But in order to keep growing in southern

A movie crew prepares to film a scene during the early days of Hollywood.

California's dry climate, Los Angeles needed water. A 233-mile (375-kilometer) aqueduct, over hills, through mountains, and across deserts, was planned. In 1913, Owens River water began to flow through the aqueduct, and the city could continue to grow.

Los Angeles's early transportation system relied heavily on electric trains. They carried passengers cheaply and efficiently and allowed the young city to sprawl across the basin and into the foothills. But the famed Red Cars would not last for long. When the first horseless carriage appeared in 1899, Los Angeles's love affair with the automobile took off with a bang and a roar. By the end of World War I, residents already noticed the brown haze of air pollution.

During this period Los Angeles grew larger and larger as it absorbed outlying communities. More people came to work in the city's varied industries, creating the need for more housing, food, clothing, schools, hospitals, and other services. And the many new residents and industries needed still more water.

In 1931, Angelenos voted to build another aqueduct to bring water from the Colorado River to the city. Begun during the Great Depression, work on this aqueduct was completed in 1939. The Depression caused some suffering in southern California, but did not stop the area's growth completely. Los Angeles built the huge Memorial Coliseum, holding 75,000 spectators, and readied it for the Tenth Olympiad in 1932. (The same Coliseum would again host the Summer Olympic Games in 1984.)

After World War II, one of the city's old problems became a highly visible one. In 1946, a St. Louis newspaper headline named Los Angeles the United States's number one "Smog Town." Yet instead of moving to solve the problem, the last electric railroads were replaced by smoke-belching buses. Over the next decades, smog and traffic congestion grew even worse.

Not all the news was bad, however. Disneyland, the first of the great theme parks, opened in neighboring Orange County in 1955, and two years later the Dodgers left Brooklyn to make their home in Los Angeles. During the 1960s, Angelenos celebrated the opening of the Dorothy Chandler Pavilion, home to music, theater, and dance.

But the problems common to any large city—traffic congestion, smog, crime, street gangs, racial tension in overcrowded inner city areas—continued to threaten its residents. In 1965 racial unrest exploded during six days of rioting in Watts, an area where many of Los Angeles's black citizens live. Thirty-four people died; thousands were wounded or arrested.

During the 1980s, battles between well-armed street gangs made headlines across America. Gang members used rapid-firing weapons to kill young Angelenos in frequent drive-by shootings.

Through all the racial conflicts, some Angelenos worked hard to encourage understanding among the city's various groups. Tom Bradley, the first black city council member, became Los Angeles's first black mayor in 1973. Bradley's successful career would keep him in public office for years to come. He and other leaders supported equal opportunity programs and an appreciation of the city's ethnic riches.

Although many of the same problems still trouble Los Angeles today,

Sleeping Beauty's castle in Disneyland.

Angelenos continue to search for solutions. To reduce dangerous levels of air pollution, the city has considered a plan approved in 1989 by southern California's regional government and smog-control agencies. This bold plan calls for changes in the life styles of most of the region's more than 12 million residents. It would encourage the use of new fuels such as methanol in automobiles and lawnmowers. Unlike gasoline, methanol does not create high levels of harmful air pollution. The plan also proposes parking fees at supermarket lots, zoning changes to move workers closer to their jobs, and limits on the number of drive-through burger stands. These measures are intended to limit the amount of air pollutants released by southern California's 8 million vehicles, in which area residents drive 234 million miles each day.

Despite the problems their city faces, most Angelenos believe that the City of Angels is the best place to live and work. And in Los Angeles, some kinds of work create play time for millions of people in the United States and around the world.

A busy freeway winds through Los Angeles.

3

Los Angeles at Work

People in Los Angeles work hard, but sometimes that work may look like fun. Angelenos are employed in an unusual variety of industries, from oil and entertainment to aerospace and financial services. The city's location and port make it important in world trade, and its sunny, mild climate and entertainment industry attract millions of tourists every year.

Los Angeles's best-known industry is probably that of entertaining the world. About three-fourths of all movies are produced in the Los Angeles area by film studios such as Columbia and Paramount. More than 60 independent studios also produce shows mainly for television. There are camera stores, film-development laboratories, costume makers, and people who rent everything from a "portable jungle" to trained tigers.

At Universal Studios, visitors watch a "Miami Vice action spectacular" staged by professional stunt performers.

A camera crew films a scene at one of the "streets of the world" at Universal Studios.

Universal Studios not only makes movies and television shows, but gives visitors a chance to view the special effects magic of show business. On the Universal tour, fans can experience avalanches and earthquakes, watch an ocean part, and be threatened by hungry sharks and giant apes.

ABC and CBS have large television studios in Hollywood. NBC has a studio in Burbank where tourists can see how sets are built, gaze at colorful costumes in the wardrobe

department, and find out how the big cameras film a show. All the networks also have free tickets available for show filmings, if visitors request tickets ahead of time and arrive early.

Many people, including highly skilled and talented professionals, work together for days to create a 30-minute television show. They include camera operators, lighting and sound technicians, make-up artists, costume and hair designers, set construction builders and designers, writers and directors, secretaries and laboratory technicians, maintenance workers, and security guards. The business of entertainment requires all these kinds of jobs and more.

With its many television, film, and radio broadcasting studios, Los Angeles is the entertainment center of the West. Los Angeles is also a center for the oil industry. Because rich pools of oil lie deep beneath the earth, oil wells can be seen almost everywhere—even on the campus of Beverly Hills High School.

The oil industry, as well as many others, is supported by the city's financial network. The World Trade Center and the Pacific Stock Exchange downtown—a smaller version of the one in New York City—as well as the many banks reflect Los Angeles's important role in world trade and finance. Because the city is located on the west coast of the United States, its trade with the Pacific Rim countries—Japan and China, Hong Kong, Korea, and others in the

Ships from around the world carry cargo through the busy Port of Los Angeles.

Orient—continues to grow.

The Port of Los Angeles in San Pedro loads and unloads more cargo than any other port on America's West Coast, more than 60 million tons each year. This total is expected to triple over the next four decades.

Once only mud flats, the port now stretches across 28 miles (45 kilometers) of waterfront, and is one of the largest harbors built by people in the world.

People as well as cargo move through the Port of Los Angeles. Big

At a McDonnell Douglas plant, workers construct a large aircraft.

cruise ships also stop here, making this the West Coast's busiest cruise center. Each year nearly a half million tourists board passenger ships for voyages to exciting places.

Other transport-related industries such as aircraft and aerospace are also important employers in the Los Angeles area. McDonnell Douglas constructs large airplanes which are sold to American airlines, and to the airlines of other countries as well. It takes many men and women months to build these modern planes.

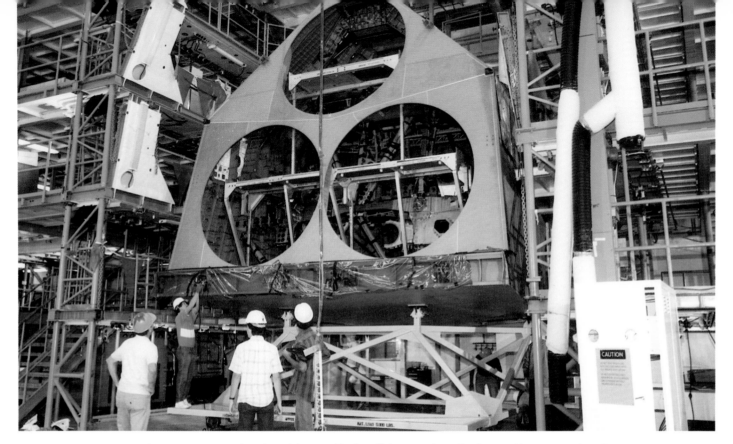

A section of a new space shuttle orbiter at Rockwell International's Space Transportation Systems Division.

In Downey, Rockwell International Corporation builds craft which fly even higher—the space shuttle orbiters used by NASA to soar far above the earth's atmosphere. Instead of earlier rockets, which could be used only once, a shuttle orbiter is boosted into space by rocket propulsion. Then, when its mission is completed, it glides back to earth like a plane and is soon ready to be launched into space again. Many workers at the Rockwell plant proudly display special license plate

holders reading, "Member—Space Shuttle team."

The Los Angeles area electronics industry produces high-technology products for space and military uses. Some electronics companies build computers, printers, and other sophisticated business machinery, while others produce computer software. Los Angeles is the nation's largest high-technology center.

The city is also the largest manufacturing center in the United States, producing everything from textiles to furniture. Although the area has many large companies, it has even more small to mid-sized firms.

Finally, tourism is one of the most important industries in and around Los Angeles. Thousands of people work in fields that provide entertainment and services for millions of visitors. Hotels and motels employ many people, as do restaurants, shops, bus and taxi companies, the many amusement theme parks, and other attractions.

Why do so many people come to Los Angeles just to have fun? Because Angelenos know how to play!

4

Los Angeles at Play

The Los Angeles area is one of the world's great playgrounds. Both nature and people have created a great variety of opportunities for fun.

Southern California's dry, subtropical weather, with little rain, mild temperatures, and frequent sunshine, makes outdoor living a local tradition. Backyard swimming pools and spas are common sights in well-to-do neighborhoods, and many apartments have balconies and decks.

Sunshine and miles of smooth beaches attract swimmers and sunbathers, while more active vacationers ride the white-capped surf or try wind surfing and beach volleyball. In early spring tourists and residents alike take whale-watching tours in search of the whales migrating along the western coastline.

Angelenos also enjoy the many

Sunbathers on a Los Angeles beach.

parks throughout the city. MacArthur Park has a small lake, playgrounds, and green grass in the center of Los Angeles. Hancock Park is the site of the La Brea Tar Pits and two museums. Exposition Park features the Sunken Garden with its thousands of rose bushes, as well as several museums and sports arenas. Griffith Park, the city's largest park, has something for everyone: wilderness areas, playgrounds, tennis courts, bridle paths, and polo grounds; an observatory and planetarium where visitors can look up at the stars and down on Los Angeles; Travel Town with trains to climb on, ride, or just observe; a Greek amphitheater; the Los Angeles Zoo; and a new museum.

Los Angeles is a city rich in museums. It would take days to see them all, and they are all worth seeing.

Downtown, the Los Angeles Children's Museum is a totally hands-on experience. Young visitors can jump on a motorcycle or pretend to steer an ambulance. They can film their friends and see the results on a nearby television screen, sing in a recording studio, cook in a child-sized kitchen, or leap and tumble atop giant, soft foam blocks.

In Exposition Park the California Afro-American Museum has displays of black history and art, while the Museum of Natural History features animal exhibits and scenes of California life at different time periods. Across the park, the Museum of Sci-

Young visitors and older ones, too, enjoy the activities at the Children's Museum.

ence and Industry offers technological exhibits and more hands-on learning.

Another museum with a chance for touching is the Cabrillo Marine Museum in San Pedro, which offers a fascinating glimpse at life in the ocean. Visitors can see swirling water in a wave tank, peer into a kelp forest, and stare at large crabs that stare back. Even more exciting is the touch tank, where a visitor can gently stroke a starfish's pebbly skin or feel a prickly sea urchin.

Angelenos who want to go from

sea animals to prehistoric animals can continue to the La Brea Tar Pits in Hancock Park. Here, they can observe the bubbling tar pools that once trapped ancient animals, and sometimes early humans as well. The George C. Page Museum holds reconstructed skeletons of some of these Ice Age victims, including mammoths with 12-foot (3.7-meter) tusks, saber-toothed cats, huge wolves, and more.

Across the park, the Los Angeles County Museum of Art includes exhibits from many different cultures and times. It has a garden filled with famous sculptures, a gallery for changing exhibitions, and a center for concerts and lectures.

One of the city's newest museums is in Griffith Park—the Gene Autry Western Heritage Museum, founded by the well-known movie cowboy. Seven galleries feature displays of different periods of life in the American West, such as native Americans, Spanish conquistadors, and American cowboys. Both the real West and the West of television and movie legend are represented.

Across from the Western Heritage Museum in Griffith Park stands the Los Angeles Zoo, considered one of the nation's finest. The zoo holds more than 100 acres (40 hectares) of landscaped terrain and 2,000 varieties of animal life. It includes a new Koala House, Children's Zoo, special shows, animal rides, and picnic areas.

Besides the parks and museums, many men and women have left their

mark on Los Angeles. One such man was Simon Rodia, who created the Watts Towers. Working alone, this Italian-born tile setter built towers from steel rods, covered them with cement, and then decorated them with broken bits of tile, glass, pottery, sea shells, and pebbles. Now considered a remarkable example of pop art, the tall towers have become a local landmark.

Somewhat better known are the actors who left their palm, foot, and sometimes paw and hoof prints in the cement in front of Mann's (once Grauman's) Chinese Theater. At this famous Hollywood landmark, tourists can examine the messages left by movie stars past and present. The nearby Walk of Fame boasts golden

The Watts Towers.

stars of many well-known entertainers embedded in the sidewalk.

Angelenos who wish to see live entertainment can visit one of Los Angeles's theaters or concert halls. The Music Center of the Performing Arts, in the city's center, includes the Dorothy Chandler Pavilion. The Los Angeles Philharmonic Orchestra performs here, and the Civic Light Opera, too. The Music Center's Ahmanson Theater, as well as the historic Pantages Theater in Hollywood and the modern Shubert in Century City, offer first-class plays.

Area residents who are more interested in sports than music have an equally wide choice. Baseball fans can follow the Dodgers—winners of the 1988 World Series—or the California Angels in Anaheim. Football fans can cheer for the Rams and the Raiders; basketball buffs can watch the world-champion Lakers and the Clippers. On the ice, the Kings are the hometown ice hockey team. Santa Anita and two other tracks draw horse-racing fans. Local sports fans also attend many college games, including special events such as the Rose Bowl. With all these sports and teams to choose from, Los Angeles fans never lack entertainment.

If Angelenos have any energy left, they can find excitement at several colorful theme parks. Disneyland, first and most famous, is located in nearby Orange County. Not as large as Disney World in Florida, Disneyland still attracts millions of visitors

Los Angeles fans cheer for the Dodgers at Dodger Stadium.

every year with new tours and rides.

Another Orange County theme park, Knott's Berry Farm, recaptures some of the rough and tumble fun of the old West. It also features cartoon characters and dinosaurs. North of Los Angeles, Six Flags Magic Moun- tain offers stomach-wrenching rides and other amusements.

Sunshine and beaches, parks and museums, musical events and thea- ters, sports and theme parks—no one ever has to be bored in Los Angeles.

5

Everyday Los Angeles

A visitor observing the busy airports, freeways, and city streets might wonder if anyone in Los Angeles ever stays at home. And where is home in this enormous, spread-out city?

Los Angeles can be divided into several areas. Downtown Los Angeles lies in the eastern half of the city. Concerns about damage from earthquakes once caused the city to limit the height of downtown buildings to 150 feet (46 meters). For many years City Hall's white tower was Los Angeles's tallest building, but in 1957 improved construction methods resulted in an end to the height limit. Now numerous skyscrapers soar upward, and even taller buildings are planned. Banks, hotels, and corporate headquarters will soon be joined by luxury apartments and more office blocks and hotels.

The skyscrapers of downtown Los Angeles.

The Civic Center, which has many government buildings, is located in the city's center. Its federal, state, county, and city offices form one of the nation's largest government complexes outside of Washington, D.C.

Downtown's L.A. Mall has two levels of shops and the Children's Museum. Shoppers looking for a bargain go to the Garment District, between Fourth and Tenth streets, or to the nearby Jewelry District. The Los Angeles Flower Market is also fun to visit. At the Grand Central Market, where signs are written in several languages, vendors sell a dozen varieties of beans and peas, and even more types of tea.

Clustered around the downtown area are many ethnic neighborhoods. Olvera Street, Little Tokyo, Chinatown, and Koreatown have interesting areas to explore.

Olvera Street is the site of the city's oldest house—Avila Adobe—as well as Mexican crafts and foods. A visitor can buy a colorful piñata there or taste spicy tacos and enchiladas. In May, Cinco de Mayo parades in many parts of the City of Angels celebrate a historic Mexican victory. Part of the El Pueblo de Los Angeles State Historical Park, Olvera Street preserves the Mexican origins of Los Angeles.

Little Tokyo, Chinatown, and Koreatown also reflect the national origins of their residents. In Little Tokyo tourists can eat sushi—raw fish—or visit a Buddhist temple. In

During the Chinese New Year celebration, people wear a dragon costume like this one in the traditional New Year's parade.

August, Nisei Week highlights the culture and history of the Japanese who came to the United States. Chinatown celebrates the Chinese New Year in January or February with parades and special events.

Some of the city's oldest neighborhoods lie on the outskirts of the downtown area. South of downtown is the Watts area where many black Angelenos live, while East Los Angeles is a low-income neighborhood settled mainly by Latino families.

Central Los Angeles, which lies between downtown and independent Beverly Hills, includes Hollywood and West Hollywood. Originally a quiet suburb, Hollywood became famous because of its close ties to the entertainment industry. Long past its heyday, today's Hollywood looks a little shabby. But from the tall "Hollywood" sign perched on the hillside to Sunset Strip with its many restaurants, nightspots, and trendy shops, this once glamorous part of the city still contains many interesting sights, as well as echoes of its past glory. Home to struggling actors and rock musicians as well as newer immigrants, Hollywood continues to attract many tourists.

Northwest of Central Los Angeles lies the San Fernando Valley. Once a quiet rural area, the valley is now filled with comfortable housing developments and dotted with backyard swimming pools. During rush hours, its freeways are crowded with commuters hurrying to and from

A typical Los Angeles area home.

other parts of Los Angeles.

North and east of downtown is the San Gabriel Valley area, which holds many small independent towns. Some are centers of business and manufacturing, such as the City of Industry; others are mainly residen-tial. Pasadena is home to the world-famous Rose Parade, held every New Year, and the Rose Bowl. San Gabriel has one of the early Spanish missions.

West Los Angeles is high-priced and fashionable. It includes Beverly Hills, Century City, Westwood, Bel

Thousands of fresh flowers are used to create a float for the annual Rose Parade.

Air, Brentwood, and Pacific Palisades. Century City, once part of a movie studio lot, is a planned community with its own office buildings, hotels, apartment houses, shopping center, and theaters. Westwood, which includes the large University of California at Los Angeles (UCLA) campus, is a youthful community with many shops, restaurants, bookstores, and movie theaters.

Beverly Hills has long been known as a community of wealth and privilege. Here, beautiful, luxurious

This elegant home in Beverly Hills is surrounded by palm trees.

homes, perfectly groomed lawns, and expensive cars are owned by successful Angelenos from many professions. Rodeo Drive, lined with expensive shops, is the world-renowned shopping street in Beverly Hills.

The South Bay area lies along the Pacific Ocean from the Santa Monica Mountains southward. It includes independent Santa Monica, with its fashionable shops and historic pier; Venice, with its canals, busy boardwalk, and artists' colony; Marina del Rey, with thousands of pleasure boats;

Houses perch along the edges of the cliffs that rise from the beach along the Palos Verdes Peninsula.

independent Manhattan, Hermosa, and Redondo Beach; and Torrance and the Palos Verdes Peninsula communities, which have comfortable homes and scenic ocean views.

At Los Angeles's southern tip lies picturesque San Pedro, including the Port of Los Angeles. Next to San Pedro stands the large city of Long Beach, with its neighboring port.

Every city neighborhood or independent community has schools. The Los Angeles County Education System includes thousands of schools

with more than a million students. They range in size from a two-room schoolhouse at one end of Catalina Island to large buildings that hold thousands of students. Since the students who attend these schools speak 85 different languages and dialects, teaching them can be a real challenge.

For higher education, Los Angeles has six community, or two-year, colleges and more than a dozen colleges and universities, both public and private. UCLA and the University of Southern California (USC) are two of the best known.

For many years Los Angeles was both admired and made fun of by the rest of the country as a place for surfers, movie stars, and strange new religions.

Today's Los Angeles is quite different. Angelenos are developing a stronger sense of their own identity, and the rest of America is taking note. Their city has become a leader in new economic and social trends, as well as in the arts and entertainment.

Los Angeles has been the model for other rapidly growing twentieth-century cities, from Denver and Dallas to Phoenix and Houston. It has also become the new door to America—the first destination for many recent immigrants who will add to the rich and varied heritage of the citizens of the United States. In these and many other ways, Los Angeles is an important center for the nation and the world.

Places to Visit in Los Angeles

Performing Arts

Dorothy Chandler Pavilion
Music Center for the Performing Arts
15th Street and Grand Avenue
(213) 972-7483

Art Museums

Huntington Library and Art Gallery
1151 Oxford Road
San Marino
(818) 405-2141

J. Paul Getty Museum
17985 Pacific Coast Highway
Malibu
(213) 458-2003

Los Angeles County Museum of Art
5905 Wilshire Boulevard
(213) 857-6000

Historical Museums

California Afro-American Museum
Exposition Park
(213) 744-7432

Gene Autry Western Heritage Museum
4700 Zoo Drive
Griffith Park
(213) 460-5698

George C. Page Museum
La Brea Tar Pits
5801 Wilshire Boulevard
(213) 936-2230

Los Angeles Children's Museum
Los Angeles Mall
310 North Main Street
(213) 687-8800

National History Museum
Exposition Park
(213) 744-3466

El Pueblo de Los Angeles State Historical
Park
Spring Street/Arcadia Street
(213) 628-1274

Science Museums

Cabrillo Marine Museum
3720 Stephen White Drive
San Pedro
(213) 548-7562

California Museum of Science and Industry
Exposition Park
(213) 744-7400

Griffith Conservatory and Planetarium
Griffith Park
(213) 664-1191

Special Places

Disneyland
1313 South Harbor Boulevard
Anaheim
(714) 999-4000

Dodger Stadium
1000 Elysian Park
(213) 224-1400

Knotts Berry Farm
8039 Beach Boulevard
Buena Park
(714) 220-5200

Los Angeles Zoo
5333 Zoo Drive
Griffith Park
(213) 666-4090

Mann's Chinese Theater
6925 Hollywood Boulevard
(213) 464-8111

NBC Studios
3000 West Alameda Avenue
Burbank
(818) 840-3537

Six Flags Magic Mountain
26101 Magic Mountain Parkway
Valencia
(818) 367-2271

Universal Studios
100 Universal City Plaza
Universal City
(818) 508-9600

Additional information can be obtained from:

Los Angeles Information Center
695 South Figueroa Street
Los Angeles, CA 90017
(213) 689-8822

Los Angeles: A Historical Time Line

1542 Portuguese sailor Juan Rodríguez Cabrillo discovers the Indian village of Yang-na and adds it to his map for Spain

1769 Gaspar de Portolá, a Spanish army captain, and Juan Crespi, a priest, stop in Yang-na and rename it *Nuestra Señora la Reina de Los Ángeles de Porciúncula*

1781 The Spanish governor of California, Felipe de Neve, offers land and supplies to families in northern Mexico to settle the land; 11 families move to Our Lady the Queen of Angels

1821 Mexico wins independence from Spain; Los Angeles becomes a Mexican provincial capital

1826 Jedediah Smith becomes the first white man to come overland to California

1841 The first group of settlers to travel overland arrives in Los Angeles

1846 Mexico and the United States begin fighting over California. United States forces capture Los Angeles in August, but are forced to leave by residents

1847 United States troops recapture the city

1848 Mexico ends war and loses California to the United States

1850 Los Angeles is incorporated as a city as California is made a state

1876 Southern Pacific Railroad links Los Angeles to San Francisco

1885 Los Angeles gets direct rail link to the East

1886	The railway fare from the Midwest to Los Angeles drops to as low as one dollar, which brings more and more people to the city	1961	Construction on Century City, a planned community, begins
1913	Owens River aqueduct project is completed	1965	Racial unrest leads to six days of rioting in the Watts area
1914	The Los Angeles harbor project in San Pedro is completed	1971	An earthquake centered in San Fernando kills 64 and causes extensive damage
1931	Construction begins on a second aqueduct to bring water from the Colorado River to Los Angeles	1973	Tom Bradley becomes Los Angeles's first black mayor; he is reelected in 1977, 1981, 1985, and 1989
1932	The Los Angeles Coliseum is readied for the tenth Olympic Games	1984	Los Angeles hosts the Olympic Games for the second time
1955	Disneyland opens in Orange County	1986	Construction begins on Metro Rail, a new subway system
1957	Dodgers move from Brooklyn and settle in Los Angeles	1989	Los Angeles replaces New York City as the largest metropolitan area in the United States

Index